Scotland in the Thirties

Scotland in the Thirties

RICHARD DREW PUBLISHING
Glasgow

First published 1987 by
Richard Drew Publishing Ltd
6 Clairmont Gardens
Glasgow G3 7LW

British Library Cataloguing in Publication Data

Kenna, Rudolph
    The thirties in Scotland.
    1. Scotland —— Social life and customs
    —— 20th century
    I. Title
    941.1083   DA772

    ISBN 0-86267-189-2

Typeset by John Swain, Glasgow
Printed in Great Britain by Butler & Tanner Ltd, Frome and London

Acknowledgments

I am most grateful to all the librarians and archivists who gave me access to their photographic collections or answered my postal enquiries. Richard Dell generously gave me permission to reproduce photographs in the Valuation Court Collection of Strathclyde Regional Archives. I owe an especial debt to Charles McKean for allowing me to use a selection of his excellent photographs of 1930s architecture.

Contents

Introduction   *page* 9
Entertainment, Sport and Leisure   21
Fashion   41
Transport   45
Architecture   57
Gala Occasions   75
Postscript   91
Index   93
Picture Credits   95

Introduction

The 1930s decade has had a very unfavourable press: it started badly with the Great Depression, and ended very badly indeed with the Second World War. In the British Isles the decade was one of deflationary economic policies, very high levels of industrial unemployment and widespread fears that unrestricted warfare would prove to be the death-knell of civilisation. There are obvious and striking parallels with the 1980s, as the 30s also produced rising levels of employment in the service section of the economy and improvements in living standards for substantial numbers of people, particularly in the new growth industries which expanded, while the old heavy industries contracted, turning out cars, motor-cycles, aircraft, vacuum cleaners, radios, artificial silk and plastics. New suburban housing estates were springing up everywhere; shiny mass-produced Ford, Austin and Morris cars were appearing on the roads in ever increasing numbers; radios and labour-saving domestic appliances were finding their way into millions of homes. In 1937 Scotland's first industrial estate was established at North Hillington, near Glasgow. By 1939 85 new factories had opened there, and another three small industrial estates had been established in Lanarkshire, at Chapelhall, Carfin and Larkhall. On the new estates the industrialist could obtain a factory on a rental basis without capital outlay; the factories were standardised and were provided with essential services. Though they did not succeed in alleviating unemployment to any considerable degree, the early industrial estates set the pattern for post-war development on a more ambitious scale.

The new world was struggling into being in the 1930s, but the period was undeniably one of glaring social contrasts: in 1933, at the height of the Depression, *The Queen* ('the Lady's Newspaper and Court Chronicle') urged its readers to insist on more than one reference when engaging a chauffeur, and the same periodical extolled the attractions of German spas, recounted the culinary adventures of 'A Gourmet on the Riviera', and advertised cruises to the Mediterranean and the Canaries. At the other end of the social scale, grinding poverty was the lot of hundreds of thousands in the 'Distressed' or 'Special' Areas of Whitehall terminology. The unemployed, many of whom were mentally or physically scarred veterans of 'the war to end wars', subsisted on a meagre dole and were subjected to a cruel and humiliating Means Test.

The conflicts in Manchuria, Abyssinia and Spain cast long shadows, but for the average man and woman the clouds of depression and political uncertainty were readily dispersed by the bright potential of Saturday Night, when Bert Ambrose, Henry Hall, Jack Hylton and Roy Fox set millions of feet tapping to music of irrepressible élan. Those were, after all, the golden years of the radio, the cinema and the *palais de danse*.

Notwithstanding wars and threats of war, hunger marches and clashes between Fascists and Anti-Fascists, the 1930s was an astonishingly productive decade — 'a brilliant age' in the opinion of one recent writer. 'Modern' was an exciting concept in the 30s, and many Scots, among them innovators of the calibre of George Bennie, John Logie Baird, Robert Watson-Watt and John Grierson, contributed towards the creative vitality of the period. The early 30s brought severe hardship, especially on Clydeside, but in the autumn of 1934 the skeletal 'No. 534', which had rusted on the stocks in John Brown's Clydebank shipyard during the two worst years of the Depression, was at last ready for launching, taking to the water as the *Queen Mary*. The *Queen Elizabeth* followed in 1938 and in that same year millions of people made the excursion to Glasgow's Bellahouston Park to savour the colour, gaiety and spectacle of the Empire Exhibition, the greatest show since Wembley (1924) and the apotheosis of the 30s in Scotland.

1

The Armistice Day service in Dundee, 1930. The Great War left scars that were slow to heal. Every year, 'at the eleventh hour of the eleventh day of the eleventh month', all traffic came to a standstill and for two minutes the nation paid silent homage to a million Empire dead. But the promise of 'a land fit for heroes' had not been fulfilled, and in the early 1930s the Depression brought misery to millions — including hundreds of thousands of Scots.

2

Junction of Argyle and Buchanan Streets, Glasgow, c. 1930. The site of the future Burton building is on the extreme right. Notice the 'Baby Austin' Seven (middle foreground), Britain's most popular small car of the interwar period; it was introduced in 1922 and remained in production until 1939.

3

The 'Girnin' Gates', Drumchapel in the early 1930s. This idyllic scene has been replaced by one of Europe's largest post-war housing estates, with a population in excess of 25,000.

12

River Clyde at Finnieston. In spite of the world-wide trade recession, the river remained an important shipping artery; passenger ships of the Anchor Line sailed regularly from Glasgow's Yorkhill Quay to New York.

Woolworth's store in Union Street, Glasgow, photographed in 1930. Its proud boast 'nothing over sixpence' had to be taken with a pinch of salt. Spectacles, for example, cost 1/6 — sixpence for the frame and an additional sixpence for each lens. Woolworth's Victory Label 7-inch gramophone records sold at 6d each and enjoyed large sales.

═══ 6 ═══

Queen's Dock, Stobcross, Glasgow. Note the preponderance of horse-drawn traffic. The giant electric crane, seen in the background, was erected in 1932 and survives *in situ*, though the Dock itself closed in 1969.

7

On hot summer days, city children were delighted by the appearance of the municipal water cart with its refreshing spray.

8

'Milk straight from the wood' in Cathcart, Glasgow (1933). By the 30s many horse-drawn vehicles had rubber tyres.

Work resumes at John Brown's shipyard (April 3, 1934). The giant hull of the future *Queen Mary* can be seen in the background. Notice the large number of men who are simply 'hanging about'. As late as 1937 15.9 per cent of the Scottish workforce was still unemployed.

The Timmer Market, Aberdeen, 1934. The last of the historic autumn fairs — a major event in Aberdeen's social calendar for centuries — to be held in the Castlegate took place on August 30 of that year. The following year the Market moved to its new site off Justice Street.

11

Gathering mussels at Ferryden, Angus (1936). Throughout the 1930s comparatively little was done to alleviate deep poverty in those areas of the British Isles that were hardest hit by the Depression. There was no American-style New Deal for the large section of the population living at subsistence level.

12

Harvesting herring at Anstruther, Fife (1939). The interwar development of new technology brought little comfort to people involved in agriculture, fisheries, textiles, and other declining sections of the economy.

═ 13 ═

King George VI and Queen
Elizabeth at Glamis Station,
April 1937. The Coronation
ceremony took place on May 12
of that year.

In terms of popular entertainment, the decade was dominated by the motion picture. The nation's Plazas, Regals, Odeons, States, Embassies and Majestics were the supreme social centres of the 1930s. A generation of children was named after the great stars. With some justification, novelist William Gerhardie referred to the movies of the golden age as 'paradise deferred'.

The super-cinema of the 30s, huge, gaily coloured, and floodlit or neon-outlined after dark, has been aptly described as the cathedral of a secular society; its quasi-religious character was enhanced by an elaborate colour-change lighting system and a powerful electric organ — which rose from mysterious depths until it was fully visible, in all its varicoloured glory, on the stage. The décor and staffing arrangements of the super-cinema were admirably calculated to bolster its unashamedly escapist role. Most of the 'supers' employed a small army of attendants — immaculately uniformed usherettes and page boys, and at least one commissionaire, dressed-to-kill in the sort of extravagantly frogged and braided creation much favoured by amateur productions of *Bitter-Sweet*.

Auditorium decorations were also designed to accentuate the fleeting delights of the silver screen — none more so than those 'atmospheric' Spanish or Moorish effects, to be found in many a suburban Toledo, Granada and Alhambra. The 'supers', some of which could accommodate 3000 people, ranged in style from quasi-Egyptian Art Deco, through Moderne to Futuristic. Their foyers and tea-lounges — usually much more subdued than their auditoriums — helped to familiarise the public with such modernistic innovations as 'abstract' floor patterns, peach and luna-blue tinted mirrors, and moulded glass lighting appliqués. The cinema incidentally provided one of the best examples of 'U' and 'Non-U' pronunciation and spelling in that class-conscious decade — 'cinema' was 'Non-U' and working or lower-middle-class, while 'kinema' was 'U' and upper-class.

Glasgow had no fewer than 98 cinemas in 1937, ranging from luxury picture palaces to 'flea-pits', and there can be little doubt that high unemployment and poor living conditions helped to account for their popularity. But the cinemas of the 30s were more than mere glorified night-shelters. With their full and varied programmes, they offered excellent value for money: full-length films, cartoons, newsreels, 'shorts', and — as an added bonus — community singing to the accompaniment of the Mighty Wurlitzer. On the anniversary of Armistice Night the organist would 'render' old favourites such as *Tipperary*, *Keep the Home Fires Burning* and *Roses of Picardy*, and there would hardly be a dry eye in the house.

While the Corinthian colonnaded auditorium of the Dundee Playhouse was in piquant contrast to its Moderne appendages, the Paramount Theatre in Glasgow's Renfield Street (F.T. Verity and S. Beverley, 1935) was Moderne throughout, with distinctive fittings in the tea-room, lounges and foyers and a superb auditorium, since destroyed through subdivision. The word 'theatre' applied to a cinema was no misnomer since the major cinemas of the 30s were also equipped with full stage facilities; many famous entertainers appeared at the Paramount.

Elstree, the 'British Hollywood', was the brainchild of John Maxwell, a Glasgow solicitor who created British International Pictures and the Associated British Cinemas (ABC) circuit. Among the memorable pre-war films made at Elstree were *Blackmail* (1929), *Music Hath Charms* (1935), *St. Martin's Lane* (1938) and *Poison Pen* (1939).

Comedies and musicals starring Will Hays, George Formby, Jessie Matthews, Gracie Fields and Jack Buchanan were among the most enjoyable British films of the decade, but it took Hungarian-born Alexander Korda to produce prestigious British films with Hollywood-style, box-office appeal — *The Private Life of Henry VIII* (1933) was one of the most popular and profitable films of the 1930s. Korda's London Films and their Big Ben trade-mark became synonymous with entertainment on a generous scale: *The Scarlet Pimpernel* (1934), *Sanders of the River* (1935), *Things to Come* (1936), *Fire Over England* (1937), *The Drum* (1938), *The Four Feathers* (1939), and *The Thief of Baghdad* (1940). The Britain of the commercial film makers seldom stretched beyond the Home Counties; Victor Saville's film version of Winifred Holtby's novel *South Riding* (1938) was a notable exception. Some of the scenes in *Shipyard Sally* (1939), a Gracie Fields vehicle, were set in a studio 'Clydebank', but the pub scene reputedly took place in Naismith's Bar in Glasgow Road, a magnificent Edwardian hostelry, demolished in the late 1970s.

Some of the most significant British films of the 30s were neither lavish spectacles nor 'quota quickies' (short, low-budget 'second feature' films). John Grierson's famous film *Drifters* (1929) inaugurated the British documentary movement, which was to be responsible for some of the most imaginative and memorable cinematographic images of the decade. In 1928 a film unit, organised by Grierson, was included among the departments of the newly-established Empire Marketing Board. The EMB only survived until 1933, but the film section was transferred to the Post Office where, as the GPO Film Unit, it continued to produce technically inventive and thought-provoking films. *Night Mail* (1936) was probably the most remarkable of the new British documentaries, but films such as *Housing Problems* (1935), *Enough to Eat?* (1936) and *We Live in Two Worlds* (1937) were if anything more influential, contributing to the climate of opinion which was to lead eventually to the creation of the post-war Welfare State.

The novelty of 'the wireless' had worn off by the early 30s, and radio had come of age. By 1932 there were 4,800,000 licence holders, and nine million by the end of the decade. The powerful luxury sets of the period were housed in streamlined Moderne cabinets of two-toned veneered walnut or moulded Bakelite. In 1935 the Murphy 'all-electric Supersonic Heterodyne receiver' cost all of £14 15s. There was no Radio 3, and in between Wurlitzer recitals, improving talks and relays of dance music, the National Programme broadcast masterworks such as *Le Sacre du Printemps* and Mahler's Eighth Symphony.

The BBC, under its first Director-General, the high-minded and austere Sir John Reith, was often accused of being supercilious and patronising. Apart from the morning service and the weather forecast, there were no Sunday morning programmes until 1938; millions accordingly tuned in to the commercial stations, Normandie, Lyons and Luxembourg.

Unlike *The Radio Times*, *Radio Pictorial*, which cost 3d and was published every Friday, was heavily slanted towards pop radio. Newspapers supplied programme details of foreign stations such as Berlin and Brussels, and staid listeners who were averse to anything remotely suggestive of jazz frequently lent an ear to Hamburg and other German stations, Nazi Germany having imposed a ban on such 'degenerate' music. Variety programmes were immensely popular, with turns such as the Western Brothers, Gracie Fields, Flanagan and Allen, George Formby, Elsie and Doris Waters and Tommy Handley. Dance music was provided by a galaxy of star bands, led by Billy Cotton, Harry Roy, Ambrose, Jack Payne, Roy Fox, Henry Hall, Jack Hylton, Lew Stone, Ray Noble and Joe Loss.

Helensburgh-born John Logie Baird invented the world's first working television and went on to pioneer transatlantic television, all-electronic colour and 3D television, and video recording. As early as 1931 owners of Baird 'televisors' had been able to view the Derby. Between 1932 and 1935 the BBC experimented with the Baird Company's low-definition, 30-line television system, and in November 1936 the Corporation inaugurated a high-definition television service which had a reception area of some thirty miles and began with alternate transmissions by two rival systems — Baird 240-line television with mechanical scanning and the all-electronic, 405-line Marconi-EMI system. In February 1937 the Television Advisory Committee decided in favour of Marconi-EMI. By 1938 the price of the cheapest television sets had fallen considerably, though at around £22 they were still very expensive, and by the following year the number of sets in use had increased to 20,000. But unfortunately for the first generation of viewers, transmission ceased abruptly on the outbreak of war and was not resumed until 1946.

In those (for most people) pre-television days, popular illustrated newspapers provided a visual commentary on the news and achieved large circulations. The weekly magazine *Picture Post*, first published in 1938, was a milestone in photo-journalism; unlike the glossy 'top people's' magazines, it showed that there was more to Britain than Royal Ascot and the Eton vs. Harrow Match. Competition between newspapers was particularly intense in the Depression years, leading to ruthless 'circulation wars' and a never-ending flow of inane gimmicks. A typical newspaper 'stunt' of the period was described by J.B. Priestley in his entertaining novel *Wonder Hero* (1933). New subscribers were canvassed on a door-to-door basis and were bribed with offers of the Complete Dickens or free life insurance. In 1933 Lord Beaverbrook's *Daily Express* overtook its rivals and reached a circulation of over two million copies, and the Express buildings in London, Manchester and Glasgow, streamlined and clad in shiny black Vitrolite, proclaimed the power of the Press in no uncertain manner.

Many readers of popular newspapers turned first to the sports pages, ignoring headlines which trumpeted Hitler's re-occupation of the Rhineland and annexation of Austria. Every Saturday, in stadiums the length and breadth of Britain, footballers in voluminous shorts were cheered on by vast numbers of raucous cloth-capped partisans. Devotees of the turf put their hard-earned sixpences on Gordon Richards, and in 1933 their idol rode no fewer than 259 winners, thereby breaking the previous record set by the great Fred Archer in 1885. But comparatively new spectator sports such as greyhound racing and speedway were also tremendously popular in the 1930s. Greyhound racing began in Manchester in 1926 and spread rapidly throughout the country; in Glasgow White City, Carntyne and Shawfield drew huge crowds, and the first totalisator, or 'tote', on a greyhound track was set up at Carntyne in 1929. Ice-skating also enjoyed a considerable vogue in the 30s, and new rinks were opened in the major Scottish Towns and cities.

The theatre — especially variety and revue — remained a major attraction throughout the 30s, in spite of the rival claims of radio and cinema. Jack Buchanan personified the elegant man-about-town and Jessie Matthews, singing 'Dancing on the Ceiling' in an engaging contralto, was the ideal girl-next-door. The Scotland of the 1930s still boasted an astonishing variety of live entertainment venues — grand theatres, historic music-halls, winter gardens and seaside pavilions. In the mid-30s the light-hearted *Half Past Eight* shows — less sophisticated, perhaps, than West End revue, but brimming over with vitality — played to capacity audiences in Glasgow and Edinburgh. The Scottish variety stage was particularly well supplied with star comedians, including Jack Radcliffe, Tommy Lorne, Harry Gordon, Jack Anthony, Dave Willis, Tommy Morgan, and — arguably the finest Scottish character comedian of the inter-war years — Will Fyffe.

The 1930s were also the golden years of British dance bands; they were heard regularly on the radio, broadcasting from top London night spots such as the Embassy Club, Monseigneur Restaurant and Café de Paris, and they occasionally visited provincial dance halls, where they met with rapturous receptions. They also made innumerable records, and it is to be regretted that the 78 rpm discs of the period were unable to do full justice to their superb artistry. Bert Ambrose, with a personal salary of £10,000 a year, was the best-paid bandleader in the world. Dance band 'crooners' such as Al Bowlly and Sam Browne made skilful use of the new electronic microphone and perfected a *sotto voce* ballad-singing style of great charm and sophistication; they were the pop stars of the era and were widely imitated by young provincial hopefuls. A number of 30s' bands were immortalised on film. In 1935, for example, Henry Hall and his New BBC Dance Orchestra appeared in the musical comedy *Music Hath Charms*. Like the super-cinema, the *palais de danse* of the 30s was rich in atmosphere; colour-change lighting and a glamorous Moderne décor greatly enhanced the pleasures of 'Saturday night at the palais'.

Keep-fit enthusiasts of the 30s cultivated the Body Beautiful by means of fresh air and plenty of exercise. Sunbathing became a cult and gave rise to popular songs such as 'The Sun Has Got His Hat On' and 'Who's Been Polishing the Sun'; the sunrise was one of the principal decorative motifs of the decade, and so-called 'sun-trap' houses with roof gardens, balconies and wraparound windows enjoyed a considerable vogue. Hikers took to the roads *en masse*, while the Women's League of Health and Beauty set out 'to epitomise the national movement in Scotland towards a fitter nation'. The first open-air mass-demonstration given by the League in Scotland took place at Westerlands, Glasgow, on June 25, 1938, the highlight of the programme being the choice of a Fitness Queen.

Cyclists and hikers were able to take advantage of country roads that were still very quiet, with — by today's standards — comparatively few private cars, and for the modest outlay of one shilling they could stay overnight in a youth hostel. Dr Allan Fothergill was the moving spirit behind the Scottish Youth Hostels Association, which was inaugurated at a public meeting in Edinburgh in February 1931. The Association's first hostel — formerly a row of farm workers' cottages — was opened on May 2, 1931 at Broadmeadows, near Selkirk. Contractors' huts, renovated and moved to new sites, also did duty as hostels in the early days. Carn Dearg in Wester Ross, opened in 1932, was the first Scottish hostel to provide a meals service.

Holiday camps were another important innovation of the 1930s, and indeed, they were to preserve their breezy 30s formula — frequent Tannoy announcements and hearty *Volksgemeinschaft* — for several decades to come. Billy Butlin's first holiday camp was opened at Skegness on Easter Saturday, 1936, and its phenomenal popularity led to the opening, in 1938, of a second holiday camp at Clacton-on-Sea. The war intervened, and it was not until 1947 that Butlin's opened a Scottish camp. Situated at Ayr, it had formerly been HMS *Scotia*, a wartime training establishment which Billy Butlin had built for the Navy.

Strange to relate, the widespread enthusiasm for sunshine and fresh air in no way diminished the demand for tobacco. The cigarette, like the cocktail, was one of the 'sophisticated' symbols of the 30s — 'Two Cigarettes in the Dark' was a hit song of the year 1934. A plentiful supply of cigarettes and pipe tobacco had helped the citizen soldiers to endure the danger, squalor and boredom of the trenches, and after the Great War, 'emancipated' women also became heavy smokers. Stage and screen celebrities and all manner of people in the public eye happily puffed away with no thought of setting a bad example. Twenty cork-tipped 'Craven A' cigarettes, 'made specially to prevent sore throats', cost 1s, and cigarette cards featuring footballers, cricketers and radio personalities were avidly collected by small boys.

Auditorium of the Ritz, Rodney Street, Edinburgh. Built by Scottish Cinemas and Variety Theatres, the Ritz was one of the first Scottish cinemas to be equipped with a sound installation. It opened on September 10, 1929, with *The Singing Fool*, an early Talkie starring the irrepressible Al Jolson.

15

The Stirling Regal on opening day. A photograph which underlines the popular appeal of the cinema in the 1930s. The cinema architect's own special blend of Art Deco was reflected in the screen Deco of many Hollywood movies.

The striking advertising tower of Green's Playhouse, Dundee (John Fairweather, 1936), as it appeared before it was up-dated by means of grey ribbed metal cladding. In the 30s its sculptural qualities were enhanced by red and blue neon. The entrance foyer and restaurant were in the Moderne style and the staircase was flanked by neon-illuminated glass panels. The opulent auditorium was designed by John Alexander of Newcastle and set 'standards of luxury unrivalled anywhere else in Scotland'.

══ 17 ══

The Commodore, Whiteinch (Glasgow). A 1196-seater, it was designed in 1931 by James McKissack and the entrance facade was clad in architectural faïence. The Commodore's original proprietor, George Singleton, later sold the cinema to Oscar Deutsch of Odeon fame. In the industrial belt of Scotland, the gaily-coloured cinema frontage of the 30s was in startling contrast to the soot-darkened stone of surrounding buildings. No fewer than 890 new cinemas were built in Britain between 1932 and 1937 — more than three a week!

══ 18 ══

The 1780-seater Riddrie Vogue (Glasgow). One of George Singleton's handsome suburban super-cinemas, opened in 1938; the architect was James McKissack. It is interesting to compare the Vogue's fluid Moderne styling with the angular early-30s idiom of the Stirling Regal.

The Regal in Lothian Road, designed by W.R. Glen, was Edinburgh's largest super-cinema at the close of the 30s decade. One of John Maxwell's ABC chain of cinemas, it opened on October 10, 1938, with *Vessel of Wrath*, starring Charles Laughton and Elsa Lanchester. In 1969 the Regal became the ABC Film Centre, with three screens. At night the super-cinema, decked out in coloured neon, shone like a beacon; hundreds of 'patrons', devotees of Hollywood glamour, formed orderly queues under the watchful eye of a smartly uniformed commissionaire.

Shipyard Sally, in which Gracie Fields averted unemployment on Clydeside by charming the powers-that-be in London, was released in 1939 and was the last film she made in the United Kingdom. Her co-star was comedian Sidney Howard (top left).

21

The staff of Hamilton's cinemas outside the La Scala, 1939. Cinemas and dance halls were among the new sources of employment in the 30s, when the service section of the economy was in a comparatively healthy condition.

22

'The Palladium of Scotland' — Glasgow's famous Empire Theatre, Sauchiehall Street, photographed in June 1930. The largest music hall outside of London; its reputation as 'the graveyard of English comedians' was greatly exaggerated.

One of the most popular radio personalities of the 30s was Henry Hall, who led the dance orchestra in the Gleneagles Hotel, Perthshire, before taking charge of the New BBC Dance Orchestra in 1932. His signing-off tune, 'Here's To The Next Time', was as familiar to hundreds of thousands of listeners as the chimes of Big Ben.

24

The incomparable Tommy Lorne. Born Hugh Corcoran in Kirkintilloch, he was brought up in the New City Road district of Glasgow. By the early 30s he was a star comedian, appearing in pantos, reviews and summer shows throughout Scotland. He died in April, 1935.

25

Debonair Jack Buchanan, Scotland's answer to Fred Astaire, was born Walter John Buchanan in Helensburgh on April 2, 1890. In 1932 he starred in *Goodnight, Vienna* alongside Anna Neagle, later to achieve fame as Queen Victoria in *Sixty Glorious Years*. Buchanan, who specialised in musical comedy roles, was a matinée idol in America as well as in this country.

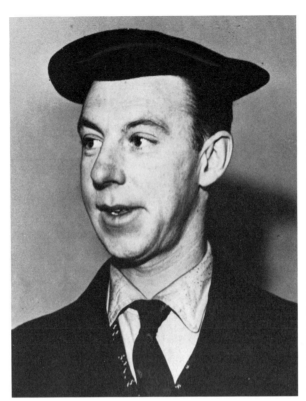 

26

Harry Gordon and Will Fyffe —
two of Scotland's premier
entertainers in the 1930s. Harry
and Will, both of whom were
superb character comedians,
were close friends and co-starred
in pantomime at the Glasgow
Alhambra.

27

An impromptu performance by
Aberdonian comedian Harry
Gordon, self-styled 'Laird o'
Inversnecky' (a mythical village
in the North-East of Scotland). In
the 30s he made hundreds of
broadcasts from Aberdeen's
Beach Pavilion, where he
produced Harry Gordon's
Entertainers from 1924 until
1940.

28

The great American golfer Bobby Jones at St. Andrews, 1930. In the summer of that year Atlanta-born Robert Tyre Jones won the Open and Amateur Championships of Britain and the United States and retired at the age of 28, having reached the pinnacle of golfing achievement. Jones, who held degrees in engineering, literature and law, played with hickory-shafted clubs throughout his career. In 1958 he was honoured with the Freedom of the Burgh of St. Andrews, where the 10th hole on the Old Course is named after him.

29

Rangers FC Scottish Cup Team 1929—30. Winners of the Glasgow Cup, Charity Cup, Scottish Cup and Scottish League Championship. The great Bob McPhail is in the front row (fourth player from the right), to this day the club's record goalscorer, with 233 goals in 354 League matches.

30

Celtic FC (1936—37). Scottish Cup Winners for the fifteenth time. The legendary Jimmy Delaney and Jimmy McGrory are in the front row (first and second players from the left). McGrory scored 397 goals in 378 League games. Although the star player of the 1930s frequently performed before 100,000 or more spectators, he seldom earned more than £8 a week. In 1937 147,365 spectators saw Celtic beat Aberdeen in the Cup Final.

31

Partick Thistle FC, 1936—37. In the 'fitba' daft' Scotland of the 30s huge gates were commonplace, and no fewer than 149,415 were present at Hampden Park for the Scotland—England match of 1937.

Benny Lynch, the first Scottish boxer to win a world title. On September 9, 1935, he defeated Jackie Brown in Manchester's Belle Vue stadium to become flyweight champion of the world. 20,000 people packed the concourse of Glasgow's Central Station to welcome Gorbals-born Lynch on his triumphal return from Manchester. On Wednesday, October 13, 1937, he retained the championship at Shawfield Park, knocking out his challenger, Peter Kane, in the thirteenth round. Lynch died in 1946 at the early age of 33.

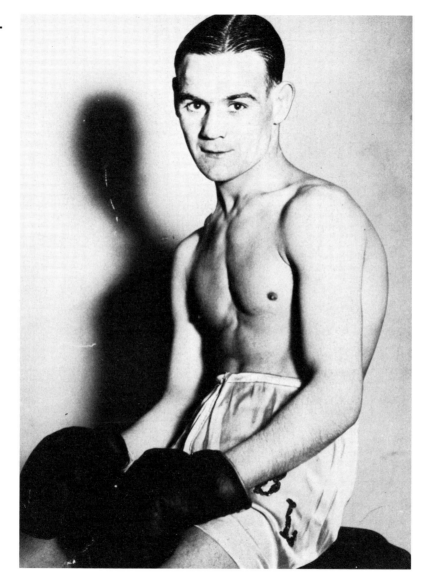

═ 33 ═

It was the decade of Mass Observation, Social Credit, the Loch Ness Monster, and Hiking! In 1933 the Duke of Kent inspected Dundee Hiking Club. Note the quasi-military style of dress, not dissimilar to that of Fascist organisations of the same period; many sporting associations of the 30s had a penchant for uniforms.

═ 34 ═

Hunt Meet at Floors Castle, Kelso, December 1935. The gulf between rich and poor yawned wide in the 1930s; Empires had toppled since 1914, but in this country the lifestyle of the privileged minority appeared to be largely unaffected by the world war and its aftermath.

Hawick Ba' Game. Note the
prevalence of the 'cloth-cap
image'.

A Scottish member of the Women's League of Health and Beauty receives tuition from the League's founder, Prunella Stack. In the 30s the League had an enormous nationwide membership. The uniform was black satin shorts, a white satin blouse and a red blazer with white piping. A hit song of the 30s advised women to: 'Keep young and beautiful, it's your duty to be beautiful'.

Fashion

In reaction to the shingled, flat-chested 'boyish look' of the 1920s, women's fashions of the 30s were extremely feminine, at their best achieving a degree of elegance which has seldom been surpassed. The stunning designs which Erté, already celebrated, continued to produce throughout the 30s, enshrined the *haute couture* ideals of the period — ideals which could, however, only be attained by the leisured and wealthy. On a less exalted plane, in cities, towns and villages throughout the land, young women modelled their appearance on the female stars of 'the Talkies' — Hollywood was a great leveller or a pernicious influence, depending on one's point of view. Jean Harlow's platinum hair earned her the epithet of 'the blonde bombshell' and led to a worldwide boom in the sales of hydrogen peroxide. In the local Odeon the working girl had access to the greatest fashion show on earth, created by indigenous Hollywood designers such as Gilbert Adrian and Howard Greer, and modelled by 'screen goddesses' such as Greta Garbo, Claudette Colbert and Joan Crawford.

Long skirts and dresses, slinky bias-cut evening gowns (the backless and sleeveless evening dress was one of the major fashion innovations of the decade) and two-piece suits were all highly representative of female attire in the 30s. The ubiquitous cloche hat of the 1920s was superceded by a wide variety of headgear, ranging from tiny 'pill-boxes', worn at a jaunty angle, to broad-brimmed 'picture' hats. The figure-hugging bias-cut dress, invented by Mme Madeleine Vionnet, was the acid-test of the female form, which had to conform to the streamlined image of the 30s. Beach pyjamas arrived from fashionable Continental resorts such as Saint Tropez and Juan les Pins, and with the craze for hiking, shorts also came into popularity. Etiquette — still a very serious consideration in the 30s — helped to account for the popularity of evening dress; an upper-middle-class couple dining alone would still dress for dinner, the husband wearing a dinner jacket and the wife a gown.

Largely due to improvements in manufacturing methods and the development of man-made fabrics such as Rayon and Celanese, inexpensive and attractive ready-to-wear clothes were widely available and were seen to advantage in multiple stores such as C & A Modes. A further development was high-quality ready-made fashions, adaptations of Paris *couture*, which retailed in leading department stores and speciality shops — some of which affected French names. Large and chunky jewellery was in vogue, the wealthier young favouring a platinum setting for their precious stones. Lips and nails were painted in bright colours, hair was Marcel-waved, and face powder, too liberally applied, resulted in many a chalky and faintly ghostly countenance; but Palmolive toilet soap helped women to retain 'that schoolgirl complexion'.

Though decidedly formal by the standards of the present day, the gent's lounge suit, shoes and soft collar of the 1930s were a considerable advance on the heavy serge suit, boots and stiff collar of the pre-1914 era, when a man's mode of attire had been an almost infallible guide to his status. For everyday wear, the well-dressed man wore a double-breasted suit with wide lapels; shirts were white or striped, with detachable collars, and polka-dot ties were extremely popular. Knitted pullovers, woollen stockings and plus-fours (voluminous knickerbockers) — in the 30s the favourite garb of golfers — were also worn as casual dress by individuals who were quite ignorant of the significance of the 19th hole. Montague Burton, Hepworth's and other similar companies were able to supply men's clothing at highly competitive prices, since they produced the garments themselves and sold them through their own multiple stores. A smart double-breasted suit, made to measure, could be obtained for 55/- — but bear in mind that a weekly wage could be as little as £2 10s!

The well-groomed man's hair was worn short, smoothed down with Brylcreem, and covered when out of doors by a soft, wavy-brimmed trilby hat. The cloth cap and muffler, on the other hand, were part of the uniform of the manual worker, and while cloth caps were also worn by golfers and other sporty types, the 'superior' article was carefully shaped to distinguish it from the proletarian 'bunnet'. Beards and other hirsute embellishments were *démodé*, with the exception of a tiny moustache *à la* Ronald Colman or Clark Gable.

Ladies' hairdresser, Pollokshaws Road, Glasgow (1937). In the 30s the permanent wave was at the height of its popularity, and setting lotions such as 'Amami' were widely used to achieve inexpensive home perms. A famous advertisement proclaimed 'Friday Night is Amami Night'.

═══38/39/40═══

Ladies' fashion shops in the Glasgow of the 30s, when the vogue for comparatively inexpensive, ready-to-wear fashions resulted in a wave of shop premises with eye-catching Moderne frontages. Kaye Ltd, Trongate (1935), Grafton's, Argyle Street (1936), and Audrey, Sauchiehall Street (1937).

Gents' outfitters in Glasgow. J & H Spencer, Argyle Street (1936) and Weaver to Wearer, Main Street (1939). With the expansion of multiple tailors, superficial class distinctions were largely eliminated: smart suits in the latest styles could be obtained on very easy terms. A 'snap brim' felt hat added the finishing touch to the well-dressed man's outfit.

In 1930 Glasgow-born engineer George Bennie demonstrated his experimental railplane on a section of test track at Milngavie, where 'a typical country railplane station' had been built sixteen feet above Burnbrae railway siding, by arrangement with the London and North Eastern Railway. The gaily-painted, cigar-shaped car, constructed at the Dalmuir works of William Beardmore & Co, was similar in design to an airship gondola and could accommodate 25 persons, all of whom were provided with armchairs, tables and reading lamps. It travelled, suspended from bogies, on a monorail supported by girders and latticed steel towers and was propelled by airscrews driven by electric motors. Lloyd George, Ramsay MacDonald and the heads of three railway companies were among the VIPs who inspected the box-girder track and travelled on board the streamlined car; seated high above the surrounding countryside they enjoyed a magnificent view of the Campsie Fells and Blane Valley and at once realised the tremendous possibilities of the revolutionary new form of transport.

Bennie's proposals for a cheap nation-wide system of monorail transport were originally developed in the early 20s, long before the days of motorways and large-scale car ownership. He believed that his railplane system could be operated in conjunction with the existing railways, with the former carrying passengers and perishable goods and the latter being largely reserved for heavy goods traffic. He further envisaged that railplane and track construction would help to reduce unemployment, providing many jobs in the steel and coal industries. Among Bennie's visionary schemes was a railplane system of transport between Glasgow and Edinburgh (with the journey being accomplished in a mere twenty minutes) and a similar link between Glasgow and Balloch; speeds of up to 150 miles per hour were anticipated. There were even proposals for a London—Paris—London—Brussels route.

The late 1920s had been a period of enthusiastic speculation concerning the City of the Future; airships and skyscrapers had caught the popular imagination, as indeed had Fritz Lang's remarkable film *Metropolis* (1926). 1930 therefore seemed to be an auspicious time in which to embark on an exciting project like the railplane, and so it might have proved had it not been for the tragedy of the Depression; by the end of the year unemployment had increased to $2\frac{1}{2}$ million. Bennie's ambitious plans were cruelly thwarted by the economic slump of the early 30s; he had sunk all his capital in his invention, and he became a bankrupt in 1937. The test track survived until 1956 — the year which preceded the inventor's death — when it was completely demolished for scrap. The Bennie railplane was far from being the harebrained notion of a crackpot inventor; in the late 20s the German town of Wuppertal already possessed a monorail system, which had been operational since the turn of the century

In the mid-30s 'the amazing new Morris ten four' (ten horse power, four cylinders) cost £172 10s ex-works. Motor taxation, based on horse-power strength, diverted demand towards the smaller, cheaper car, and by 1935 over 60 per cent of new cars sold in Britain were of ten horse power or less. The average retail price of cars dropped by about 50 per cent between the mid-1920s and the mid-1930s, and by the end of the decade petrol was 2d per gallon cheaper than in 1914! With the remarkable growth in private car ownership came the Road Traffic Act (1934) which instituted driving tests and a 30 mph speed limit in built-up areas. In 1933 Percy Shaw made night-driving safer by inventing 'cat's eyes', while Leslie Hore-Belisha, Minister of Transport from 1934 to 1937, gave his name to the 'Belisha beacons' which alerted motorists to the presence of pedestrian crossings.

Symbolic of the new age of private motoring was the roadhouse. Some roadhouses were merely converted country houses, but many others were purpose-built in sleek Moderne fashion. Edinburgh's new roadhouse was designed in 1935 by Patterson and Broom for a Leith firm of restaurateurs and was advantageously sited on Maybury Road, Corstorphine, within a stone's throw of the Edinburgh—Glasgow highway. Another luxurious Scottish roadhouse of the 30s was the Hollywood Hotel, opened in 1937. Situated on the Greenock Road, about a mile from Largs, it had sixty bedrooms, spacious lounges and public rooms, a conference hall and a swimming pool. A sun verandah ran the full length of the building, and the 330-feet Moderne-style frontage was rendered in Snowcrete; the architect was Thomas G. MacLachlan of Ayr. With their cocktail lounges and dance-floors, roadhouses had a trendy, up-market image, and patrons were more likely to drive up in Alvis or Frazer-Nash sports cars than in humble 'ten fours'.

In the interwar period the 'paleotechnic age' of Patrick Geddes was rapidly giving way to the 'neotechnic age' of Lewis Mumford; the transition was symbolised by the great airships with their impressive, but flawed, technology, and by locomotives such as the *Silver Link* and *Duchess of Rutland* — beautifully streamlined, but powered, like the *Rocket*, by steam. The LNER initiated the streamliners in 1935 with the 'Silver Jubilee' service between London and Edinburgh. The train was hauled by A4 Pacifics, the most famous of which was the *Mallard*, now preserved in the National Railway Museum at York. On July 3, 1938, on a special test run, it momentarily touched 126 mph, a world speed record for a steam locomotive. The LNER *Coronation* (London—Edinburgh) and the LMS *Coronation Scot* (London— Glasgow) were both introduced in 1937. The *Coronation Scot* was hauled by streamlined Stanier Pacifics; on its first passenger-carrying trials between London and Crewe in June 1937 it raised the speed record to 114 mph. The previous record was held by the *Silver Jubilee*, which reached 113 mph in August 1936.

In 1931, at Daytona Beach, Malcolm Campbell captured the world land speed record, travelling at 245 mph, a feat for which King George V knighted him. Four years later, at Bonneville Flats, Sir Malcolm achieved a speed of 300 mph. He then turned his attention to the water speed record. The first of the *Bluebird* hydroplanes was built by Saunders Roe and equipped with the old Rolls-Royce engine from the *Bluebird* racing car. First tests on Loch Lomond in 1937 revealed a number of faults, and *Bluebird* was later taken out to Lake Maggiore where Sir Malcolm achieved a world water speed record of 128 mph. At Lake Coniston in 1939, in a second *Bluebird* hydroplane with a new Rolls-Royce engine, he pushed the world record up to 141 mph.

It was in July 1930 that the total of British unemployed exceeded two million for the first time, rising to over three million at the height of the Depression. By 1935 the workless total — just over two million — was the lowest for five years; Scotland's unemployed total had fallen below 300,000, and Glasgow had fewer than 100,000 out of work. For many people the Cunard White Star liner *Queen Mary*, setting out on her maiden Atlantic crossing to the strains of 'Auld Lang Syne', was a tangible symbol of national recovery. The great ship left Southampton on May 27, 1936, on

the birthday of the Queen whose name she carried. Among the passengers were a team of reporters and commentators from the BBC, and band leader Henry Hall, who was responsible for the *Queen Mary's* official signature tune — 'Somewhere at Sea'.

The hull plate of 'Job No. 534' had been laid on December 1, 1930, but work had ceased on December 11, 1931, and had not restarted until the morning of April 3, 1934, when the Dalmuir Parish Pipe Band had led the workers into the yard to where the skeleton of the ship — with some 80 per cent of the hull plating completed — lay encrusted with 130 tons of rust. The launching ceremony took place on the afternoon of Wednesday, September 26, 1934. In August 1936 the *Queen Mary* won back for Britain the Blue Riband of the North Atlantic, completing the crossing in 3 days, 23 hours and 57 minutes, beating the previous record set by the French liner *Normandie* by several hours. The British liner lost the Blue Riband to the *Normandie* the following year, but regained it in 1938 and held it until the post-war era.

Unlike the Orient Line's *Orion* (1935), which was decorated in a subdued modernistic manner, the *Queen Mary* was a floating Deco palace, resplendent with choice veneers, flashed opal glass, tinted mirrors, silvered bronze and python-skin fabrics. The artificial lighting was particularly effective, much use being made of continuous trough lighting, moulded glass appliqués and illuminated pylons of onyx or enamelled metal. The ballroom was equipped with a system of automatic colour-change lighting, similar to that installed in super-cinemas of the same period.

In September 1938 grandstands were erected on the opposite side of the river from John Brown's shipyard and hundreds of thousands of people gathered to see the *Queen Mary's* sister ship being launched by Her Majesty Queen Elizabeth. At 83,673 gross tons, the *Queen Elizabeth* was the world's largest liner, but when she eventually made her maiden voyage it was in conditions of secrecy — the great ship sailed to New York where she was to receive the finishing touches before serving as a troopship for the duration of the Second World War.

George Bennie (in bowler hat) at Burnbrae, Milngavie, where he demonstrated his experimental railplane on 426 feet of test track (April 1930). It was in the field of transport that the 30s decade gave full expression to its delight in all things sleek and modern. Speedboats, racing-cars and record-breaking aeroplanes such as the De Havilland 'Comet' *Grosvenor House*, were welcomed as trailblazers of an exciting new era, and in the remarkable 'World of Tomorrow' series of Mitchell's Cigarette cards, innovations such as the Bennie railplane and Short-Mayo Composite aircraft were featured along with rockets, manned spacecraft and other long-range forecasts.

45

In 1933 the Morris Six Special Coupé could be obtained for £265. The 30s were perhaps the golden years of motoring: cars had become comfortable and reliable, while unspoilt countryside lay within easy reach of the towns and cities. Between 1930 and 1937 the number of private cars registered in the United Kingdom rose from just over one million to 1,834,248.

46

In the 30s family motoring was epitomised by cars such as this Rover saloon (1934), but stylish luxury cars such as the S.S. Jaguar '100' and the Daimler *Straight Eight* also graced the roads in that decade of 'conspicuous consumption'.

Art Deco staircase in the Maybury Roadhouse, Corstorphine (Patterson and Broom, 1935). Many roadhouses were distinguished by a rather flashy, sub-Hollywood glamour. The typical roadhouse of the 30s was a combination of pub, hotel, restaurant and recreation centre; some were equipped with swimming pools. They were the haunt of sophisticated souls who disdained the rustic pleasures of the old-fashioned country pub.

Bookstall in Glasgow's St. Enoch Station, photographed in August 1936, when *John Bull* and the *Boy's Own Magazine* were still going strong, and the redoubtable Sexton Blake, aided by intrepid boy-assistant Tinker, was tracking down evildoers in the *Union Jack*. But the brilliantly successful *Picture Post* would not appear on station bookstalls until October 1938.

Moderne styling applied to a steam locomotive — the streamlined *Coronation Scot* (1937), which operated a six-and-a-half hour service between London and Glasgow. In the 30s locomotives were frequently cited as examples of 'fitness for purpose'. The Chrysler *Airflow* was another famous example of 1930s streamlining, but the practice was often dictated by aesthetics rather than function: streamlining was *chic* and was applied to stationary objects such as cocktail bars, cinemas and radios.

Rutherglen's Main Street in March 1936. In the 30s almost every important street was etched with tramlines, though the tram-driver's reign as 'king of the causeway' was almost over.

Edinburgh tram driver. In 1937 the Scottish capital had 26 electric car services; the last tram ran in November 1956.

═ **52** ═

Corner of West Nile Street and Sauchiehall Street, Glasgow, in the late 1930s. Notice the elegantly streamlined *Coronation* tramcar, introduced in 1937. At its peak between the wars Glasgow's impeccably-run tramway system was the second largest in the UK.

═ 53 ═

Sir Malcolm Campbell at the controls of the first *Bluebird* hydroplane, Loch Lomond, 1937. Each of Campbell's racing cars and speed boats was named *Bluebird* from the play *L'Oiseau Bleu* by Maurice Maeterlinck. After the Second World War he experimented with jet-propelled boats.

═ 54 ═

The Short—Mayo Composite aircraft on the River Tay, October 1938. The brainchild of Major Mayo of Imperial Airways, the Composite consisted of *Maia*; an S.21 Empire flying boat, and *Mercury*, an S.20 seaplane. *Maia* carried *Mercury* into the air, where the seaplane was released to fly with full fuel tanks to its destination. Between November of 1938 and the outbreak of war, the Short-Mayo Composite operated a non-stop mail service between Southampton and Egypt.

The *Queen Mary* ready for launching. During her career she would make 1,000 commercial trips across the North Atlantic and carry over two million fare-paying passengers. Known as '534' because 533 ships preceded her at John Brown's yard, she was built with the help of a Government subsidy of £9½ million.

Avant-garde architects of the 30s expressed admiration for ships and locomotives, and the deck architecture of the great liners was reflected in the sun decks and white tubular railings of seaside pavilions and other Moderne building types.

On September 27, 1938, 50,000 spectators in John Brown's yard saw HM Queen Elizabeth launch 'No 552' and name the ship *Queen Elizabeth*. The King had been obliged to remain in London on account of the international crisis. The glamour associated with the great *Queens* could not altogether obscure the fact that the world no longer looked to this country for the bulk of its shipping tonnage. In 1909—13 Britain had produced nearly 60 per cent of world tonnage; in 1938 only 34 per cent.

Architecture

The commercially acceptable Moderne style of the 30s was a *mariage de convenance* between Art Deco and Modernism. Figured veneers, tinted mirrors, neon and fluorescent lighting fixtures, Bakelite, Formica, Vitrolite and chromed metal were among its principal ingredients, and it was probably seen at its best in cocktail bars, smart restaurants and expensive shops. Many writers and social commentators deplored the new fashion, variously decribing it as 'vulgar', 'tawdry', and 'meretricious'. Yet like it or loathe it, Moderne was symptomatic of a new boldness in architecture and interior decoration, of optimism and self-confidence, all of which would lead in due course to 'the cult of the new' which pervaded the 60s and 70s.

Moderne was not, however, wholly restricted to commercial premises. The Firestone and Hoover buildings in London and the India Tyre and Rubber factory at Inchinnan were among the most successful applications of the style and were designed by Wallis, Gilbert and Partners. The India Tyre factory's main office building on Greenock Road (1930) was modelled on the central pavilion of the magnificent Firestone factory on London's Great West Road (1929; demolished 1980). The two-storey frontage was stuccoed in white, with quasi-Egyptian decoration in coloured faïence.

In its heyday the ambivalent Moderne style was never quite respectable architecturally, unlike International Modern — altogether more 'highbrow', and not at first very popular. By their very nature 'utilitarian', hospitals, schools and factories were able to make the transition from Traditional to Modern without greatly offending public susceptibilities. The influence of the flat-roofed Continental Modern house with its horizontal glazing, sun terrace and white-rendered exterior was seen at second hand in the pavilions of the new schools and hospitals of the 30s. Hawkhead Hospital at Paisley (1938) was originally an infectious diseases hospital, built at a time when tuberculosis, diphtheria, scarlet fever and whooping cough were still illnesses to be reckoned with, and the six ward pavilions were entirely self-contained. The administration block, pavilions and nurses' home were in the International Modern style, with flat roofs and white rendering; the architects were Sir John Burnet, Tait and Lorne.

Scotland's most prominent building of the 1930s was St. Andrew's House (1934—39), designed by Thomas S. Tait, and built on the site of Edinburgh's old Calton gaol. The Calton Hill site was a magnificent one, and the building's heavy masses dutifully expressed the majesty and dignity of Government; some of the architectural detail was, however, undiluted 30s Moderne. The principal facade was decorated with six symbolic figures, executed by Sir William Reid Dick and representative of *Architecture, Statecraft, Health, Agriculture, Fisheries* and *Education*. The Royal Coat of Arms of Scotland above the main entrance was the work of Alexander Carrick RSA. The bronze doors, symbolic of St. Andrew's Cross, were designed by Walter Gilbert and were opened for the first time in October 1939. St. Andrew's house has often been criticised for the concessions which it makes to academic classicism; there is, however, reason to doubt whether an uninhibited exercise in International Modern would have fitted in quite so successfully with the traditional character of the Scottish capital; certainly the new St. Andrew's House in the St. James's Centre more closely resembles the proverbial grim fortress of bureaucracy.

Among Edinburgh's most adventurous commercial buildings of the 1930s were Jay's premises in Princes Street (1938), designed by T.W. Marwick, with sculptural enrichments by Thomas Whalen. The same architect was responsible for the National Bank of Scotland in George Street (1938). Leslie Graham-Thomson designed the Caledonian Insurance Company head office in St. Andrew Square (1939), a steel-framed building with outer walls of brick, a facing of granite, and an attic storey faced with bronze sheeting. The marble columns flanking the entrance support bronze figures by Alexander Carrick.

An important feature of city life in the 30s was the imposing café-restaurant with dining facilities on several floors. The London firm of J. Lyons & Co had pioneered the multi-storeyed restaurant in the 1920s and their famous Corner Houses, designed by Oliver Bernard, had incorporated some spectacular decorative effects. In the first-floor restaurant of the Corner House in Tottenham Court Road, the wall surfaces presented a vast panorama of Niagara Falls, executed in veneers of varicoloured marble. There were many handsome multi-storeyed restaurants in 1930s Glasgow, erected by leading catering firms such as R.A. Peacock & Son Ltd and James Craig Ltd. They were essentially democratic in character, with cafés and restaurants of varying degrees of refinement under one roof, offering everything from a light snack to a slap-up meal. While some were conservative in style, others were more enterprising, with a wealth of Art Deco and Moderne motifs. Henderson's Angus Restaurant in Argyle Street, opened in December 1938, was highly representative of the type, with a gents' smoking-room in the basement, a bakery sales and confectionery department on the ground floor, the 'Glenesk' first-class dining room (where a four-course luncheon cost 12s) on the first floor, the 'Kinnaird' popular dining room on the second floor, and the 'Glamis' suite — incorporating a ballroom and lounge — on the third floor. The Angus Trio Orchestra performed daily in the 'Kinnaird' room.

In the 30s — long before the days of package holidays — millions ventured no further than local resorts; beaches were strewn with people in various stages of undress, for the sun cult was in the ascendant, and suntan was *chic*. Many seaside towns invested in handsome new pavilions and hotels, some of which struck an appropriately nautical note, with strong horizontal lines, porthole windows, tubular metal handrails, sun decks and gleaming white rendering. Some of the most attractive beach pavilions of the late 30s showed the influence of the famous de la Warr Pavilion (1934) at Bexhill-on-Sea, designed by Erich Mendelsohn and Serge Chermayeff. Rothesay's modernistic municipal pavilion was designed by James Carrick of Ayr, and the same architect was responsible for the municipal pavilions at Gourock and Dunoon. Seaside pavilions were designed to function as dance halls, conference centres and summer variety show venues; like their exact contemporaries, the super-cinemas, they are nowadays more frequently used for bingo.

Portobello's magnificent open-air bathing pool was opened in May of 1936. The massive complex featured heated salt water, a wave-making machine, underwater lighting, shutes, springboards, and a concrete tower with five diving stages. There was an extensive terraced area for spectators, and the main range of attractive Moderne-style buildings was painted cream, set off by green and blue. In the course of one pre-war summer's day, no fewer than 18,000 people, bathers and spectators, passed through the turnstiles at Portobello.

Flat-roofed concrete or cement-rendered dwellings, influenced by Continental 'machines for living in', began to appear in these islands in the early 30s, and some enterprising speculative builders cheerfully adapted or bowdlerised the new architecture. In 1935 Messrs D. Hogarth and Sons of Ayr were offering flat-roofed bungalows of white Snowcrete construction for £700. Most home buyers, however, settled for the traditional bungalow with pitched roof; the vast majority were reasonably well-built, though some leaded glass in an angular Deco pattern was frequently the only concession to the modern spirit. In the Scotland of the mid-30s a five-apartment bungalow of traditional construction could be purchased for £850, or 29s weekly.

House interiors, if sufficiently up-to-date, were characterised by light pastel colours and new types of furniture and decorative accessories, such as built-in electric fires, frameless mirrors, low circular glass-topped tables, and cocktail cabinets. Some of the finest furniture of the 1930s was produced for the commercial market by Heal and Son and designed by Ambrose Heal. The firm's wide range of dining room, living room and bedroom suites, featuring such fashionable innovations as curved, light-coloured veneers and chromed metal supports, enabled the owner of a modern house or flat to furnish *à la mode* at a fraction of the cost of purpose-made, architect-designed furniture.

The trend was in the direction of labour and space saving ideas. *Bric-à-brac* was largely eliminated, but the prevailing simplicity was occasionally set off by a chromed metal statuette or a ceramic wall mask, cellulose-finished in bright colours. By 1935 Art Deco, formerly exclusive and redolent of exquisite craftsmanship, had been wedded to industry and was influencing the design of everything from ashtrays to wallpaper. Tiled fireplaces — stepped in the ziggurat fashion that was one of the hallmarks of 30s Moderne — replaced the carved and pelmet-draped wooden fireplaces of the late-Victorian and Edwardian era, and panelled doors were given a fashionable smooth surface by means of plywood. Tube lighting, nowadays more usually associated with business premises, was in vogue for living rooms, kitchens, bedrooms and bathrooms. 'You've Got To Be Modernistic' was a hit song of the year 1930, and throughout the decade the exponents of commercial modernism certainly did their utmost to 'jazz things up a bit', not always with satisfactory results. Among the acceptable substitutes for complete refurnishing were two or three 'abstract' rugs, some geometric-patterned curtains and a brightly coloured, angular tea-service, decorated by Miss Clarice Cliff.

The kitchen was the place where there ought, in principle, to have been least resistance to innovation, but many 30s kitchens were drab utilitarian places with dreary colour schemes and few if any built-in fitments; a considerable number were still dominated by huge cast-iron ranges. The modern kitchen, such as it was, would at least have been equipped with a gas or electric cooker and a water heater such as the popular gas Ascot; it might also have had a stainless steel sink and work top and tiled walls. An important feature of the new cookers of the 30s was the enamelled finish which eliminated the age-old chore of blackleading. An electric washer with wringer attached could be obtained for 15 guineas, and in 1938 Glasgow Corporation Gas Department was offering 'a refrigerator from 1/8 a week'.

The post-war shortage of domestic servants reconciled many members of the prosperous middle classes to living in flats — service flats for preference. Flat-dwelling, however, was far from being a novelty in Scotland — as early as the eighteenth century, the citizens of Edinburgh, rich and poor, had rubbed shoulders in the lofty tenement 'lands', and tenement architecture (not necessarily a contradiction in terms) had made a unique contribution to the townscape of Victorian and Edwardian Scotland. Residential flats of excellent quality were erected in the late 1930s in both Glasgow and Edinburgh. Sandringham Court (1939) on the Broom Estate was designed by W.A. Gladstone for builders Mactaggart and Mickel; rates and services were included in the annual rent of £250. The development known as Ravelston Garden (1937), near Murrayfield golf course, was designed by Neil and Hurd and consisted of 48 spacious flats in 3 blocks of 16 flats each. The four-storey blocks, butterfly in plan, were provided with passenger lifts and roof gardens and were placed in echelon formation in order to give all the residents an unrestricted view. The service courts were enclosed by garage wings, and the external brickwork was rendered in a smooth cement finish. Kelvin Court, bordering Glasgow's Great Western Road, consisted of two huge blocks of service flats, brick-faced, with artificial stone dressings and Moderne detail. The flats, completed shortly before the outbreak of war, were designed by J.N. Fatkin for Messrs Alex. Woolf Ltd, a Newcastle firm of builders and contractors.

Wartime Britain had promised the returning servicemen 'homes fit for heroes to live in', and large numbers of Government-subsidised 'council houses' were eventually built, though not nearly enough to satisfy the demand. John Wheatley, who held office as Minister of Health in the first Labour Government, was responsible for a Housing Act which greatly expedited the construction of houses which working people could afford to rent. In 1937 Glasgow had a population of 1,119,813. The population figures for Edinburgh and Dundee were, respectively, 466,817 and 177,711. Much of the population of these and other Scottish towns and cities was concentrated in slum districts; in 1938 the Department of Health had estimated that some 45,000 houses unfit for habitation were still occupied.

The interwar municipal housing estates varied considerably in size, layout and design, and though often criticised at the time on aesthetic grounds, they have, on the whole, worn remarkably well. In Scottish towns and cities the tradition of the three or four-storey tenement was perpetuated in concrete or cement-rendered brick, and there were also many estates of two-storey block houses, set in tiny gardens and influenced by the pre-1914 garden suburb movement. From the point of view of the people who were re-housed, the principal advantage was relative freedom from overcrowding. In 1935—36 a national survey by Scottish local authorities had revealed that there were 259,559 overcrowded houses — 22.6 per cent of the houses surveyed. The corresponding figure for England and Wales was 3.8 per cent. In these circumstances, a three-apartment flat, consisting of two bedrooms, living-room, bathroom and kitchenette (complete with gas-fired laundry boiler and glazed earthenware sink) might well have appeared to be the ultimate in gracious living. Some municipal housing estates reflected the prevailing taste for strong horizontal lines, flat roofs and balconies, but no Scottish local authority saw fit to undertake a development on the heroic scale of the Quarry Hill Estate in Leeds. The major drawback of all too many of the new municipal housing estates was the deplorable dearth of amenities such as shops, cafés, cinemas and pubs; in Glasgow, for example, the City Fathers would not allow pubs on Corporation housing estates.

57

'Scotland's Whitehall' under one roof — St. Andrew's House, Calton Hill, Edinburgh, designed by Thomas S. Tait and completed in 1939.

58

Caledonian Insurance Co Building, St. Andrew Square, Edinburgh (Leslie Graham-Thomson, 1939). The Cippollino marble columns support bronze figures by Alexander Carrick, RSA.

59

With its verandahs, reinforced concrete canopy and solarium, the Cubicle Block of Hawkhead Hospital — originally designed for separating doubtful infectious diseases — reflected the avant-garde ideas of the Continental Modern School. The architects were Sir John Burnet, Tait and Lorne (1936).

60

Child welfare and health clinic in Rutherglen's King Street, designed in 1937 by burgh engineer Hugh Inglis. The upper storey was largely devoted to TB patients and contained facilities for ultra-violet ray treatment. Health centres, factory canteens and pithead baths were among the many products of 1930s' social welfare — a frequently neglected aspect of the decade.

61

Chirnside School, Borders (Reid and Forbes, 1938). Pronounced horizontal lines and extensive glazing distinguished the new schools of the 30s. Under the provisions of the 1936 Education Act, the school-leaving age was to be raised to fifteen in 1939 (a measure ultimately postponed owing to the outbreak of war), and many new schools were built to accommodate senior pupils.

The Chemistry Institute at Glasgow University, a reinforced concrete-framed building with infill of patterned brick, was designed by Professor Harold Hughes in 1937. Interwar Britain lagged far behind other advanced Western countries in the provision of institutions of technical and scientific education, though by the late 1930s determined efforts were being made to catch up. As late as 1938–39, however, only a quarter of all the degrees awarded in the UK were in scientific and technological subjects.

63

North-east extension of Templeton's Carpet Factory (1936). The architect, George Boswell, was also responsible for the colourful, faïence-decorated extension fronting Glasgow Green. With their clean lines, horizontal glazing and occasional decorative motifs in brick or faïence, Moderne industrial buildings of the 30s broke decisively with the grim tradition of 'dark satanic mills'.

The Municipal Pavilion,
Argyle Street, Rothesay (1938).
James Carrick, the Pavilion's
architect, was influenced by
Erich Mendelsohn's seaside
pavilion at Bexhill, a seminal
work of the 1930s.

The main stairs, Rothesay Pavilion. Until the late 1930s only a small fraction of the working population had holidays with pay, but in 1938 new legislation granted a week's paid holiday a year to all industrial workers.

The 30s decade was the Indian summer of many Scottish holiday resorts, but the sun cult, which flourished in the 1930s, ultimately had an adverse effect on the fortunes of towns such as Rothesay; after the Second World War sun worshippers were able to take advantage of package holidays abroad.

The open-air bathing pool at Portobello, which opened on May 30, 1936, was one of the largest in Europe, with fifty thousand square feet of heated salt water. In the 1930s band music was relayed to the pool by land line from Princes Street Gardens.

This drapery warehouse in Glasgow's Bridge Street, photographed in March 1939, typifies the commercial Moderne of the 30s; it was designed in 1935 by SCWS architects.

46a Dick Place, Edinburgh, designed by William Kininmonth and Basil Spence in 1933, lacks the metal window frames of the exemplary 30s Moderne house but is otherwise true to type. The wraparound glazing, roof gardens and light-reflecting surfaces of Moderne houses gave expression to the decade's love affair with the sun. A feature of many new houses of the period was a sun lounge fitted with 'Vita-Glass', through which beneficial ultra-violet rays could pass.

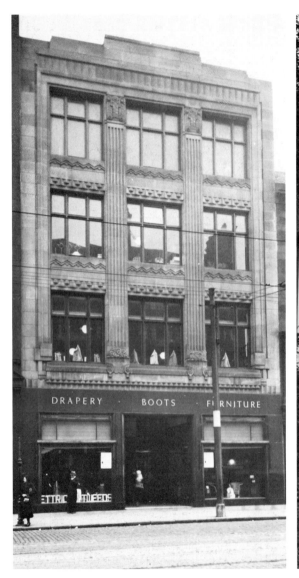

Bedroom fireplace (c. 1935), Craigie Hall, Rowan Road, Glasgow. In the 1930s tiled and stepped fireplaces were among the most popular concessions to the modern spirit. Here the use of Vitroflex has resulted in an attractive faceted-mirror effect.

Ingleneuk, Arbroath (Gordon and Scrymgeour, 1935). Note the railed balcony and the external stair to the sun terrace. Some Moderne houses clearly reflected the influence of the great ocean liners — in the 30s the most prestigious form of transport.

Miners' housing of the 1930s: Beech Crescent, Westquarter, Lanarkshire. A model of the Westquarter housing estate was on show in one of the Scottish Pavilions at the Empire Exhibition.

Living room in three-apartment house, Westquarter.

Municipal Housing, Rosemount Square, Aberdeen; begun in 1938 and designed by City Architect Albert Gardner. Notice the delightful Art Deco relief above the archway. The huge Karl-Marx-Hof in Vienna was a prototype of public housing in high density flats, but in this country, working-class housing was never as forbidding in scale.

Gala Occasions

Empire Day (May 24 — the anniversary of Queen Victoria's birth) was a major festive occasion in the 1930s, marked throughout the Empire with pageants, recitals and the inevitable renditions of 'Land of Hope and Glory'. The Silver Jubilee of King George V (May 6, 1935) and the Coronation of King George VI (May 12, 1937) were celebrated throughout Scotland with parades, processions, displays, bonfires, fireworks and floodlighting. These festivities, however, were eclipsed by the Empire Exhibition of 1938, when Glasgow was *en fête* for the first time since the International Exhibition of 1911.

His Majesty King George VI performed the opening ceremony in the city's Ibrox Stadium on Tuesday, May 3, a day of brilliant but fitful sunshine. The organisers had predicted that between May and October upwards of 15,000,000 people would make the pilgrimage to the Exhibition grounds in Bellahouston Park, but as it turned out, the actual figure was much lower; atrocious weather and the alarming international situation (the British fleet was mobilised on September 28, and war seemed inevitable until the conclusion of the 'Munich agreement') may well have discouraged many potential visitors. Among the celebrities and personalities who put in an appearance were Gracie Fields, Eddie Cantor and the Aga Khan.

Among the principal features of the Empire Exhibition were avenues devoted to the colonies and dominions, a lake 400 feet long, huge Palaces of Industry and Engineering, a concert hall, and a vast amusement park, the attractions of which included a Krazy House — with two mechanical cats screeching and meowing on the roof — a Midget Town (with real midgets), a Big Wheel, a scenic railway and a Stratoship ('direct from Chicago to Bellahouston'). 'Auto trucks', in which the passengers sat back-to-back, took the strain out of sightseeing. The architect-in-chief was Thomas S. Tait and the associated architects included J.A. Coia, Basil Spence, Launcelot H. Ross, T.W. Marwick and Esmé Gordon. Tait was responsible for the imaginative layout in which the park's dominant feature — an elongated and well-wooded hill — was left more or less in its original state, serving as a splendid foil to the Exhibition's palaces and pavilions.

The Atlantic Restaurant and the Garden Club were set on the steep slopes of the hill while the all-metal observation tower — officially entitled 'the Tower of Empire', but more popularly known as 'Tait's Tower' — dominated the crest. Designed by Thomas S. Tait in collaboration with Launcelot H. Ross and structural engineer James Mearns, it was the focal point of the layout, 300 feet in height, with two 18-passenger lifts, and the galleries at the top could accommodate 600 people. 'Tait's Tower', blue and silver under the floodlights, was strikingly futuristic and would not have looked out of place in Alexander Korda's film version of *Things to Come*. Two giant staircases, incorporating waterfalls, cascades and concealed floodlights, converged on the tower from the north and south. In the Tree-top Restaurant, located at the base of 'Tait's Tower', and elevated on steel columns, mature trees were retained as 'living decoration' and appeared to be 'growing through' the restaurant's concrete floor; the effect was strangely Surrealistic and had, moreover, a historic precedent in Paxton's Crystal Palace, which had also enclosed a number of living trees.

The *Architectural Review* considered that Bellahouston marked 'a final departure from the monumental clichés of the Beaux Arts school', while the *Architects' Journal* described it as 'the best designed Exhibition which has yet been held in Britain'. Mechanical spray painting and the use of synthetic materials such as wall board, plaster board and asbestos cement had resulted in gaily coloured, light, and obviously temporary exhibition structures, and these came as a revelation to many people who had personal recollections of the solid and unimaginative pavilions at the previous Wembley Exhibition. An integrated colour scheme was carried out in paint, floodlights, flowers and banners; the Palace of Engineering was finished in steel grey and steel blue; warm cream and red shades had been chosen for the Palace of Industry West, while the Women of Empire Pavilion was painted in pastel shades of rose and cream, the interior being finished in French grey — 'a colour chosen, after consultation, as being kindest to feminine complexions'. The pavilions of the dominions and colonies were generally considered to be the Exhibition's least successful buildings. An exception was George J. Miller's South African Pavilion, in the style of the homesteads of the early Dutch settlers. The varicoloured floodlighting of pavilions, fountains and cascades was designed to produce magical effects on warm summer evenings, and was a great success in spite of cold, wet and thoroughly unseasonable weather, which literally put a damper on the festivities.

The Garden Club (T.W. Marwick and T.S. Tait) was a private social club and contained lounge and cocktail bars, a restaurant, dance-floor and tea-terraces. It was set on the south slope of Bellahouston Hill, at the top of a monumental flight of stairs on the axis of the Mosspark entrance, and variations in level were a feature of the interior. A colonnade, through which the public had access to the top of the hill, linked the Club with a glazed rotunda containing shops. The building was lightly constructed of timber and building board and was finished in shades of cream and brown, with external sculpture by Hugh Lorimer and Thomas Whalen. The Atlantic Restaurant (T.W. Marwick and T.S. Tait), situated on the western slope of the hill, was managed by representatives of the Anchor Line and was whimsically nautical — like a parody of 30s seaside architecture — with masts and bunting and a tea-terrace modelled on an ocean liner's prow; the restaurant itself had a curved front like a deck-house.

The ICI Pavilion, designed by Basil Spence, was one of the Exhibition's most striking features. It consisted of a circular exhibition hall, with mural panels and ceiling decoration by Donald Moodie and Robert Westwater. Encompassing the hall were three triangular pylons; representative of *Earth*, *Air* and *Water*, and decorated with sculpture by Thomas Whalen, they were braced together with curved rods of cupro-nickel and were supplemented by a free-standing pylon in cupro-nickel, copper and brass. At the front of the building there was a pool embellished with stylised frogs, modelled in sheet copper by Walter Pritchard.

The Empire Exhibition came to an end at midnight on Saturday, October 31, 1938; the attendance for the last day reached 364,092, surpassing the attendance for the last day of the Wembley Exhibition. It was raining, as usual, as enormous crowds danced the 'Lambeth Walk' then converged on the South Bandstand for the relay of 'Auld Lang Syne'.

The crowds stood in silence to hear loudspeakers announce the farewell message of the Spirit of the Exhibition: 'I am the embodiment of all that made for Glasgow this memorable achievement...I live tonight; I die tonight. May memories of me abide in your hearts'. These moving words were followed by a relay of Big Ben chiming midnight in London, and in the glare of searchlights the Exhibition flag was slowly lowered. The searchlights were then switched off: the show was over.

The searchlights and the ensuing blackout presaged unpleasant things to come. Shortly after the outbreak of war the proud tower that had been a shining symbol of 1930s Scotland was removed from the crest of Bellahouston Hill; it was feared that such a prominent landmark would function as a navigational guide for enemy bombers. Half a century later, only the Palace of Art (Launcelot H. Ross) survives *in situ*; ironically, it was one of the Empire Exhibition's least adventurous structures.

Children's procession at Culter,
Aberdeenshire, in honour of the
Coronation (May 12, 1937).

Their Majesties the King and Queen *en route* for Ibrox Stadium and the official opening of the Empire Exhibition.

78

Ibrox Stadium, May 3, 1938.
Sixty thousand people were
present as HM the King opened
the Empire Exhibition.
The King's speech was relayed to
the Exhibition grounds in
Bellahouston Park.

79

'Tait's Tower' was clad in silverised steel sheeting and made a sensational addition to the Glasgow skyline. By night powerful floodlamps bathed it in brilliant illumination and the three observation balconies were edged with bands of red, green and yellow high-intensity lighting.

80

The Tree-top Restaurant formed the base of 'Tait's Tower' and had seating accommodation for approximately 400 people. One of the trees can be seen 'growing through' the Restaurant's concrete floor.

The Atlantic Restaurant, situated high on the western slope of Bellahouston Hill, was the Empire Exhibition's *de luxe* restaurant, with seating for approximately 100 people. It featured a full-size ship's bridge, complete with wheel, gyrocompass and sounding apparatus. The upper part of the building was carried over a roadway which skirted the hill.

The interior of the Atlantic
Restaurant. The Empire
Exhibition boasted seven
licensed and seven unlicensed
public restaurants, in addition to
a number of private restaurants.

The Empire Exhibition viewed from 'Tait's Tower'. The Palace of Industry is on the extreme right. Dominions Avenue and Colonial Avenue can be seen on opposite sides of the ornamental lake.

The South Staircase leading to the Garden Club; it divided near its base and gave way to a series of cascades. The Garden Club (T.W. Marwick and T.S. Tait), one of the Empire Exhibition's most successful buildings, was finished in shades of cream and brown, with external sculpture by Hugh Lorimer and Thomas Whalen. The central colonnade allowed the public to gain access to the top of the hill and 'Tait's Tower'.

Art Deco fountain in the entrance hall of the Garden Club.

85

The United Kingdom Pavilion. Designed by Liverpool architect Herbert J. Rowse of Mersey Tunnel fame, it contained four remarkable halls, identical in shape, with high parabolic roofs; stylised bronze lions flanked the entrance. There was another conventionalised lion at the head of the lake which linked the Dominion and Colonial Avenues.

88

The spectacular Exhibition amusement park, which covered 16 acres, was created and operated by master showman Billy Butlin, and involved an outlay for Butlin's of £225,000. One end of the park was dominated by a hundred-foot-high scenic railway, complete with snow-capped peaks, and the huge Dodgem track could accommodate fifty cars.

89

People who remember the Empire Exhibition generally recall with particular pleasure the quaint little vehicles — known as 'auto trucks' — which took the strain out of sight-seeing; the passengers were seated back-to-back.

The South Band Enclosure with its cantilevered canopy was designed by Thomas S. Tait. It lay on the axis of the principal avenue, immediately in front of the Palace of Engineering. For many, enjoyment of the Empire Exhibition was marred by the international crisis of August—September 1938, though spirits rose again with the pronouncement of 'peace in our time'.

Decorative veneers on display in the West African Colonies Pavilion. Veneers were widely employed in the creation of 1930s Moderne interiors.

The ICI Pavilion (Basil Spence)
aglow against the night sky.
The sculptural enrichments, by
Thomas Whalen, were symbolic
of *Earth*, *Air* and *Water*.

Postscript

'Perhaps we may escape war after all,' declared Prime Minister Neville Chamberlain in the House of Commons on the night of August 29, 1939. The previous day, many thousands of Scottish schoolchildren had rehearsed the evacuation procedure, marching from their schools to the nearest railway stations. On August 31 the British Government decided to complete naval mobilisation and to call up the Regular Army Reserve. The work of fortifying towns and cities against air attack was stepped up; public buildings and communications posts such as police boxes were screened with sandbags, and tenement closes were reinforced with steel struts. Twenty-five hostels owned by the Scottish Youth Hostels Association were taken over by the authorities to accommodate children evacuated from Glasgow, Edinburgh and Clydebank.

On September 1, the day on which Germany invaded Poland, the three-day evacuation of children began, priority being given to children from heavily-industrialised areas. In some cases as early as 6.30 am, schoolchildren and younger children accompanied by their mothers assembled with their haversacks and gas-masks and proceeded by bus or train to reception areas which had officially been classified as 'safe'. That night Britain experienced the black-out for the first time; steel-helmeted police and special constabulary patrolled the streets warning householders to observe the black-out regulations, and ARP personnel maintained a 24-hour vigil.

At 11 am on September 3 the Anglo—French ultimatum expired and Chamberlain announced that the country was at war; all cinemas, theatres and other places of entertainment were closed 'until further notice', and school was cancelled 'for the Duration of the Emergency'. But much to everyone's surprise, Armageddon failed to materialise on cue: no all-out assault with high-explosive and poison gas, no mass casualties, no panic-stricken mobs, no looting and famine. Instead, the interval of the 'Phoney War' enabled Great Britain to build up her air defences, something she would have been unable to do had it not been for the scientific and technological breakthroughs of the 1930s, that Janus-like decade which brought 'such welcome and unwelcome things at once' and which seems in retrospect to have been one of the watersheds of the twentieth century.

93

Evacuees departing from Lochee Station (Dundee) in September 1939. Each child is equipped with a gas mask in a cardboard container: in the 30s it was taken for granted that poison gas would be the decisive weapon in any future war. The Government issued 38 million gas masks, and there were special Mickey Mouse and Donald Duck masks in bright colours for tiny tots.

94

Pupils of Dundee's Harris Academy arrive at Brechin, September 1939. Experts had forecast some 300,000 civilian casualties in the first month of hostilities, and it was widely believed that at least half a million Britons would die in air raids within hours of war being declared.

Index

Italicised numbers refer to illustrations

Adrian, Gilbert, 41
Alexander, John, 26
Ambrose, Bert, 9, 22-23
Anthony, Jack, 23
Archer, Fred, 22
Art Deco, 57-58
Associated British Cinemas, 21, *28*
Audrey, ladies' outfitters, 43, *40*

Baird, John Logie, 9, 22
Beardmore, William & Co., 45
Beaverbrook, Lord, 22
Bennie, George, 9, 45, 47, *43-44*
Bernard, Oliver, 57
Beverley, S., 21
Bluebird, racing car and hydroplanes, 46, 54, *53*
Boswell, George, 65
Bowlly, Al, 23
British Luma Lamp Factory, Glasgow, 66, *65*
Broadmeadows, youth hostel, 23
Broom Estate, Glasgow, 59
Brown, Jackie, 37
Brown, John & Co., 46
Browne, Sam, 23
Buchanan, Jack, 23, 32, *25*
Burnet, Sir John, Tait and Lorne, 62
Butlin, Billy, 23, 87

Caledonian Insurance Company, Edinburgh, 61, *58*
Campbell, Sir Malcolm, 46, 54, *53*
Carrick, Alexander, 61
Carrick, James, 58, 67
Chamberlain, Neville, 91

Chemistry Institute, Glasgow University, 64, *62*
Chermayeff, Serge, 58
Chirnside School, Borders, 63, *61*
Cliff, Clarice, 58
Coia, J.A., 75
Commodore cinema, Glasgow, 27, *17*
Coronation, LNER express train, 46
Coronation Scot, LMS express train, 46 locomotive, 51, *49*
Cotton, Billy, 9
Craig, James, Ltd., restaurateur, 57
Craigie Hall, Glasgow, 71, *71*
Delaney, Jimmy, 35, 30
Deutsche, Oscar, 27
Dick, Sir William Reid, 57
Duke of Kent, H.R.H., 38, *33*
Dundee Hiking Club, 38, *33*

Empire Exhibition (1938), 9, 75-76, 80-90, *79-92*
Empire Theatre, Glasgow, 30, *22*
Erté (Romain de Tirtoff), 41

Fairweather, John, 26
Fatkin, J.N., 59
Fields, Gracie, 29, *20*
Flanagan and Allen, 22
Formby, George, 22
Fothergill, Dr. Allan, 23
Fox, Roy, 22
Fyffe, Will, 23, 33, *26*

Garden Club, Empire Exhibition, 76, 84, *85,* 85, *86*
Gardner, Albert, 74

Geddes, Patrick, 45
George, David Lloyd, 45
Gerhardie, William, 21
Gilbert, Walter, 57
Gladstone, W.A., 59
Glen, W.R., 28
Gordon, Esmé, 75
Gordon, Harry, 23, 33, *26-27*
Gordon and Scrymgeour, 72
Grafton's, ladies' outfitters, 43, *39*
Graham-Thomson, Leslie, 61
Greer, Howard, 41
Grierson, John, 21-22

Hall, Henry, 9, 22, 31, *23,* 46
Handley, Tommy, 22
Hawkhead Hospital, Paisley, 62, *59*
Hays, Will, 21
Heal, Ambrose, 58
Hogarth, D. and Sons, builders, 58
Holtby, Winifred, 21
Hore-Belisha, Leslie, 45
Howard, Sidney, 29, *20*
Hughes, Professor Harold, 64
Hylton, Jack, 9, 22

I.C.I. Pavilion, Empire Exhibition, 76, 90, *92*
India Tyre and Rubber Factory, Inchinnan, 57
Industrial estates, 9
Ingleneuk, Arbroath, 72, *72*
Inglis, Hugh, 62

Jones, Bobby, 34, *28*

Kane, Peter, 37

Kaye Ltd., ladies' outfitters, 43, *38*
Kelvin Court, Glasgow, 59
King George VI, H.M., 20, *13,* 75, 78, *77*
Kininmonth, Sir William, 70
Korda, Alexander, 21
Krazy House, Empire Exhibition, 75

La Scala cinema, Hamilton, 30, *21*
Lang, Fritz, 45
Lorimer, Hugh, 76, 84
Lorne, Tommy, 23, 32, *24*
Loss, Joe, 22
Lynch, Benny, 37, *32*

MacDonald, James Ramsay, 45
MacLachlan, Thomas G., 45
Mactaggart and Mickel, builders, 59
Marwick, T.W., 57, 75-76, 84
Matthews, Jessie, 21
Maxwell, John, 21, 28
Maybury Roadhouse, Edinburgh, 45, 49, *47*
McGrory, Jimmy, 35, *30*
McKissack, James, 27
McPhail, Bob, 35, *29*
Mearns, James, 75
Mendelsohn, Erich, 58, 67
Milk Marketing Board, Glasgow depot, 66, *64*
Miller and Black, 66
Miller, George J., 75
Moodie, Donald, 76
Morgan, Tommy, 23
Mumford, Lewis, 46

National Bank of Scotland, Edinburgh, 57
Neagle, Anna, 32

Neil and Hurd, 59
Noble, Ray, 22
Normandie, S.S., 46

Orion, R.M.S., 46

Paramount Theatre, Glasgow, 21
Patterson and Broom, 45, 49
Payne, Jack, 22
Peacock, R.A. and Son, Ltd.,
 restaurateurs, 57
Picture Post, 22, 50
Playhouse cinema, Dundee, 21, 26, *16*
Portobello bathing pool, 58, 69, *68*
Priestley, J.B., 22
Pritchard, Walter, 76

Queen Elizabeth, Cunard White Star liner,
 9, 46, 56, *56*
Queen Elizabeth, H.M., 46, 20, 13
Queen Mary, Cunard White Star liner, 9, 46,
 55, *55*
Queen's Dock, Glasgow, 15, *6*

Radcliffe, Jack, 23
Ravelston Garden, Edinburgh, 59
Regal cinema, Edinburgh, 28, *19*
Regal cinema, Stirling, 25, *15*
Reith, Sir John, 22
Richards, Gordon, 22
Ritz cinema, Edinburgh, 24, *14*
Ross, Launcelot H., 75-76
Rothesay Pavilion, 58, 67-68, *66-67*
Rowse, Herbert J., 86
Roy, Harry, 22
Rutherglen health centre, 62, *60*

Saville, Victor, 21
Shaw, Percy, 45
Short-Mayo Composite (*Maia* and *Mercury*),
 54, *54*

Singleton, George, 27
South Band Enclosure, Empire Exhibition,
 88, *90*
Spence, Basil, 70, 75-76, 90
Spencer, J. & H., gents' outfitters, 44, *41*
St. Andrew's House, Edinburgh, 57, 60, *57*
St. Enoch Station, Glasgow, 50, *48*
Stack, Prunella, 40, *36*
Stone, Lew, 22

Tait, Thomas S., 75-76, 84, 88
'Tait's Tower', Empire Exhibition, 75, 80,
 79
Templeton's Carpet Factory, Glasgow, 65,
 63
Timmer Market, Aberdeen, 18, *10*
Tree-top Restaurant, Empire Exhibition,
 75, 80, *80*

United Kingdom Pavilion, Empire
 Exhibition, 86, *87*

Verity, F.T., 21
Vionnet, Madeleine, 41
Vogue cinema, Glasgow, 27, *18*

Wallis, Gilbert and Partners, 57
Waters, Elsie and Doris, 22
Watson-Watt, Robert, 9
Weaver to Wearer, gents' outfitters, 44,
 42
West African Colonies Pavilion, Empire
 Exhibition, 89, *91*
Western Brothers, 22
Westquarter, miners' housing, 73, *73-74*
Westwater, Robert, 76
Whalen, Thomas, 76, 90
Wheatley, John, 59
Willis, Dave, 23
Women's League of Health and Beauty,
 23, 40, *36*

Woolf, Alex. Ltd., builders, 59
Woolworth, F.W. & Co. Ltd., Glasgow, 14,
 5

Youth hostels, 23

Picture Credits

	plates		plates
Aberdeen City Libraries	10, 76	Glasgow Museums and Art Galleries; Rutherglen Museum	50, 60
BBC Hulton Picture Library	49	Mitchell Library, Glasgow	43-44
Central Regional Archives	73-74	Mrs Jean Yuill	36
Charles McKean Esq	47, 57, 59, 61, 70, 72, 75, 82-83, 86, 89, 91-92	National Film Archive	20
		National Monuments Record of Scotland	58, 62-63, 66-67, 71, 79, 81, 85, 87
D.C. Thomson & Co Ltd	1-2, 4, 6-9, 11-13, 23-35, 45-46, 51-54, 56, 77-78, 80, 84, 88, 90, 93-94	Singleton Holdings Ltd	18
		Scotsman Publications Ltd	19, 68
		Scottish Film Archive	14-15, 17, 21
Dumbarton Libraries	3, 55	Strathclyde Regional Archives	5, 22, 37-42, 48, 64-65, 69